The Trunk

by Ed Casey

illustrated by Anthony Accardo

SRA
McGraw-Hill

Columbus, Ohio

A Division of The McGraw·Hill Companies

SRA/McGraw-Hill

A Division of The McGraw·Hill Companies

Send all inquiries to:
SRA/McGraw-Hill
250 Old Wilson Bridge Road
Suite 310
Worthington, OH 43085

ISBN 0-02-674292-6
  2 3 4 5 6 7 8 9 SEG 00 99 98 97

A  .

trunk

3

A .

wig

He is a .

clown

A  .

badge

She is a  .

police officer

 Boots .

He is a  .

firefighter

 and a  .

Overalls   hat

She is a  .

farmer

 and  .

Crowns   capes

He is a  .   She is a  .

king   queen